Holding my Breath
Watching from the sidelines of addiction

Laura Swash

ACKNOWLEDGMENTS

Thank you to all those from STaRS (Essex Specialist Treatment and Recovery Service) and from Open Road drug and alcohol support services in Colchester, UK who helped and befriended Colin for so many years. All profits from this book are for them.

Thank you also to my husband Uwe and my children and grandchildren who accepted my brother Colin as he was.

This writing is dedicated to Colin, and all those who knew and loved him, and is especially for his son and family.

CONTENTS

INTRODUCTION

The person beneath the addiction

My brother died on November 20th, 2019 of pneumonia complicated by his drug and alcohol addiction. He was sixty-three years old, my only sibling and I miss him. I hope this book will help others who have relatives and friends who live with substance dependence. It is a personal story of how I tried over the years to walk along the cliff edge between supporting Colin without actively enabling his addiction and without losing his love and friendship completely by rejecting him. I found ways to suspend judgement long enough to be of help, but also failed sometimes to differentiate successfully between my need for 'big sister' control and his need for self-respect and independence. Though of course he was never truly independent. His drug and alcohol needs saw to that.

Writing has been cathartic for me, but it is also a way of recording, before I forget it, a story that would otherwise be lost. I am sure many of you will have had similar experiences to the ones I recount. I have kept advice to a minimum, have just written about what I found helpful and have included a list of useful contacts at the end. The sub-headings to each chapter are a summary of a lesson learnt. Maybe reading about my struggles with Colin's addiction will allow you to feel better over what you could or couldn't do, for your friend or relative or what you are still doing for them. I have changed names where necessary to protect the privacy of Colin's other relatives and of those friends who are still alive.

Unlike a lot of similar books, there is no happy reprieve for Colin who didn't 'come to his senses' and suddenly realise where he was heading. Nearly all of his friends were addicts and he had attended more funerals that he cared to remember. He knew where his future lay, but felt helpless, and always hoped he would be the exception.

While this book's focus is on my brother, every addict's needs affect their family and friends. Standing by and seeing a loved one's health deteriorate due to their own behaviour is difficult, and it often feels easier to walk away. So, I don't apologise for also focusing on my feelings, because I have spoken to others enough to know that this is a struggle that many of us are going through daily. Holding my breath is what I have been doing for a large part of my life: while I waited for bad news; while I wondered what to do as I tried to make allowances for what I couldn't comprehend; and while I felt the most extreme frustration that any progress Colin might make was always temporary and quite quickly reversed.

Feeling conflicted and confused was common. I respected my brother's humour, his intellect and his kindness. But his grubby appearance and generally unkempt look embarrassed me. Wasting money on haircuts and clothes was not on his agenda. Using the cleaning materials I provided also depleted his energy, and the mop and bucket I bought him stood unused in the corner of his flat unless I wielded it. The sticky floors, his grimy bathroom and his beer-splattered bedroom all combined to make me feel guilty that I wasn't continually cleaning up and yet resentful at his neglect of what was originally an airy, light and welcoming home. Sometimes I spent my time cleaning while chatting to him, but usually I acknowledged it as a hopeless task. I always hugged him hello and goodbye, knowing at each visit that it was important to hide my churning fear for him and smile and chat normally to this dear man with whom I shared so many memories.

Eventually I stopped blaming myself for not being able to keep Colin's health from deteriorating and instead ensured that every visit was a pleasant one. I hired a car when I came over from my home in Portugal three or four times a year and increased my phone calls to several a week when I was away. When I visited we went out to the countryside, to the pub, to the shops, and to the hospital. I would find out when Colin had his hospital appointments and time my visits to coincide, so at least he kept some of them.

I got used to the space people quickly made for us - the empty seats next to Colin in waiting rooms and the way they moved aside on the pavement to let us through. I shrugged and thought about how I would feel when there was no Colin beside me. For my younger brother, with his addiction to alcohol, cannabis, crack cocaine and heroin (or for a few years methadone), was clearly very ill. And self-induced illness is still debilitating and miserable. Over the years he was diagnosed with Hepatitis C, chronic obstructive pulmonary disease (COPD), severe anaemia and liver damage. He suffered a series of mini-strokes and increasingly frequently from uncontrolled nosebleeds that made his flat look like something out of a horror film, the last one leading to his admission to hospital for two days a few months before he died.

This short stay in hospital was further complicated by him persuading his partner Denise to smuggle in some beer. She told me that she hadn't been able to resist his pleading. However, he drank this down as fast as he could, and then vomited so violently that his nose bled again and his discharge was delayed. By the time I was deciding to fly over, Colin was home with his nostrils packed with cotton wadding and a doctor's appointment to have this removed. He just took it out himself after a few days. Typically, my brother blamed the recurrent nosebleeds on a cauterization he'd had done when he was a small boy, and not on the perforated septum and other damage he had caused his nose by persistently snorting cocaine for over thirty years!

As well as missing hospital and doctors' appointments Colin would also often refuse the diagnostic tests he needed. He had problems with swallowing in his last two years and lost weight rapidly, weighing about seven and a half stones (under 50 kg) at the end of his life. Several doctors removed him from their lists as a waste of their time, and he took this as yet more proof that it was hopeless turning to the medical profession. He didn't really want to know what was wrong with him and nor, he felt, did they.

He tried a few times to give up alcohol without any support and suffered excruciating stomach pains and collapse, which convinced him even more that he needed to drink. If your loved one ever tries this, warn them off it. It is very dangerous and can result in seizures and strokes. Of course Colin needed to drink, just as he would need help to give up. He was both psychologically and physically dependent and would need a lot of medical support to be able to get off the drink, more so than the heroin, which methadone could help with. His disorganisation and haphazard approach to life made this impossible. He needed residential care while he dried out, and he was never at a point where he wanted to try this. At that time, I wasn't aware of the many organisations available to help, some of which are listed at the end of this book. But really, the only person who could help my brother was Colin himself

After his death, I found hospital letters to his most recent doctor - the one who had refused to come out and see him two weeks before he died. They had been worded medically, but copied to Colin, stating that they had been unable to investigate his 'possible carcinoma' further as he refused to have the endoscopy and colonoscopy that they wanted to conduct. I understood why. By this time, considering his tiny, fragile frame, these procedures must have seemed unendurable for him.

Could I have done more? Possibly, yes. Did I know what that 'more' was? Definitely not. But maybe this book will be of use to those who have relatives like my brother who seem a hopeless case but are, after all, just a person living in their own very difficult way.

Colin, 2008

CHAPTER ONE

WHERE TO BEGIN?

Childhood memories bind you together

It's hard to know where to begin, except in the very recent past, which provides such a striking contrast to Colin as a young child. As we strolled to the corner store for his 'tinnies' one day, I paused for Colin to catch his breath and I was suddenly transported back in time by a vivid childhood memory. Running through the hedged footpath connecting our house to the shops, despite my long legs, I was the one gasping behind my seven-year-old brother, who dashed ahead laughing at me. He was a speedy runner as a little boy, arms and legs pumping as he sprinted to the end of the path. There was only twenty months between us in age, but I was tall while he was tiny, leading adults to assume at least a three-year gap. Old ladies smiled and commented how 'sweet' Colin was, while I was a 'big girl' in charge of my brother. Always a good girl, always looking after him and always to blame for any trouble he managed to get into as he ran ever faster away from me!

Our different characters already visible. March 1957

Colin was a charming child, with an angelic and yet mischievous smile and incredible resources of energy. The youngest and tiniest in any sports team he chose to join, he nonetheless ran rings around those twice his size. He was everybody's friend. Even in his last few years of life, my brother would somehow summon reserves of energy to give anyone any help that it was in his power to offer. I was horrified to visit him about a year before his death and find him in extreme pain with bruised ribs from a fall suffered when trying to help his upstairs neighbour carry a wardrobe. Colin had offered assistance and had ended up at the bottom of the stairs with the cupboard on top of him. And no, he wouldn't hear of going to the doctor.

Back to 2018, and Colin paused on the way to the shop and reached in his side pocket for his inhaler. 'Trouble is,' he wheezed, 'You need breath to take these damn things.' He winked, gave up on the inhaler and lit the second half of a ciggie instead. We ambled on, lost in our own thoughts.

Short-sighted, dreamy and always with my nose in a book, I was labelled as the 'academic' one. For, although he was bright Colin was much too restless to do well in class at the local primary school. Instead, he used to escape from the playground at break and at lunchtime, establishing an early pattern of disliking school, hating any authority, and running faster than those who would try to catch him. I was posted by the front gates of the school at breaks and lunchtimes to prevent this, in which I was mainly unsuccessful, as he scaled the low wall instead! However, a pattern of supervising and being responsible for him was developed early in me. Looking after Colin was my job.

He joined the Cub Scouts soon after I joined the Brownies. I loved being a 'helpful gnome', but Colin soon found a group of like-minded friends who stole their parents' cigarettes and lit up in the long grass at the back of the scout hut, until caught and expelled by Akela. I remember our father's shame as he tackled the Cub leader demanding an explanation for Colin's expulsion - and got the truth. There were quite a few 'black sheep' in our mother's side of the family, and to me it seemed clear that Dad thought this was to blame, with Colin's inheritance of family bad blood already evident. However, a few months ago, while doing a little research on our family tree I discovered that our paternal grandfather's birth certificate from the late nineteenth century listed no father, and he had been born out of wedlock. This grandfather was also a notorious drinker and gambler, though he managed to hang onto the family business. Colin and I were both really scared of him when we went to visit and were always banished into the dimness of the front room to play with the box of shells and keep quiet. I have begun to think that our father's narrow attitude to raising children and his disgust at Colin's addictions had much deeper roots in shame at his own father's birth and behaviour.

I continued to try and be well-behaved enough for both of us. And in the face of our father's silent anger and our mother's long-term depression and ill-health, my little brother and I formed a tight alliance and defended each other fiercely, each feeling truly loved only by the parent of the opposite sex.

My brother persisted in smoking from the tender age of nine or ten years old, while our father gave up cigarettes after a long struggle. Our mother's excellent sense of smell led to her accusing Dad of cheating. His indignant denial resulted in Colin's discovery, as he leant out of his bedroom window, flicking his butts onto the flat roof of our shed. A few years later, Mum was also the one to find the cannabis resin in the chest of drawers in his bedroom. She told me, but not our father, as she was always concerned to protect my brother. Not that Dad ever raised a hand to us. Revolted by his own father's drinking, gambling and beating of his four sons, our father was a teetotal non-gambler who used silence and the threat of rejection to try and control his children. And so, by the time he was about thirteen or fourteen years old, Colin was already spending his pocket money on brown paper bags of five cigarettes and stealing money from around the house for dope. Our mother covered for him; our father didn't cotton on till later. It ruined his relationship with Colin for ever.

Like our father, Mum also never drank except for the occasional sherry at Christmas time. But she took Valium for her 'nerves' from the 1960s onwards until her death in 1991 at sixty-seven years old. Our family life revolved around her failing health, as she struggled with depression, obesity, rheumatoid arthritis, diabetes, breast cancer and heart disease. Looking back now, I can see that conversations with parents and some understanding on both sides were sorely lacking. Everything was a 'front', and a lot went on behind it.

Colin and I laughed together some time back when we realised that our claustrophobia was a result of being forced as children to hide in the coat cupboard under the stairs with our mother whenever there was a thunderstorm, or whenever anyone unknown knocked at the door. It took years for either of us to be able to go in a lift, and I always hesitate before answering the door.

Colin and I diverged in our responses to growing up in an emotionally repressed household. I became a smiling, chatty and rather nervous young girl who, until my wilder teens, tried to do everything to please our parents and my teachers. I escaped into books and my imagination, when I wasn't keeping out of the way physically by hiding in the garden. Top at school, helpful around the house (though this was not without resentment), I was only happy when gaining the approval of others. In contrast Colin became cheeky and very lively and hard to control, hiding his mischief behind an innocent face.

Once he hit his teenage years, the atmosphere between Dad and him became ever more electric, as Colin refused to get out of bed on weekends, avoided washing as much as possible, and spent his time out with friends whom my parents never met. The final crisis came when I left home and school at sixteen, refusing to fulfil the 'good girl' role anymore. Colin had lost an ally, and he quickly confided that he would leave too as soon as he could.

Fewer than two years later Colin enjoyed tinkering with motor bikes, staying out late, smoking, and drinking. He managed to fail all his O-levels except for Art. Soon after that he also left school and home. The final break with our father came when he lost a crane-driving job with the army, because a random locker check had found his amphetamines. Looking back, it is strange that I seem not to have blamed Colin for his drug-taking. I understood that we both had our different escapes.

I suppose, though, that our childhood seemed at least from the outside to be reasonably normal for a middle-class family at the time, in that we were well fed and dressed and attended school regularly. Our parents were very careful with money, but along with his younger brother, Dad had inherited his family's tyre-fitting business, and indulged us with horse-riding lessons and eventually half-shares in ponies. He loved horses, and we loved riding. It had the added benefit of getting us out of the house and away from our mother's rather unpredictable temper. Not that this was ever mentioned as an underlying reason!

Colin was an excellent rider and at one time suggested he would like to train to be a jockey. With his tiny, wiry frame he would have been ideal, but evidently one of our father's customers who could have helped Colin get into this took one look at my brother's feet and declared he would grow too tall. This turned out to be false, as he grew to just five feet six inches and never weighed more than nine stones (about 57 kgs). But our father took this advice as the end of the matter, and Colin was persuaded not to pursue his ambition. He mentioned this several times later in his life as a lost opportunity and I wonder if it would have made any difference. But, given that Colin was already smoking cannabis at fifteen and beginning to look rather unkempt, I suspect our father's acquaintance may have had other reasons for taking a step back.

Saturday mornings were sometimes tricky in our household. This was when Mum was at home alone with us, an unusual occurrence. I had started school as soon as I was four years old in order to take the strain of childcare from her, and Dad would be home from work soon after 5 pm every evening, so she was only on her own with both us children for one or two hours a day at most, and we learnt to keep out of her way if things looked a bit stormy. We spent the majority of our school holidays playing at our maternal grandmother's house. She lived next door, and even when she and our mother weren't talking to each other, we children would creep secretly through the holes we made in the hedge to visit Nana.

However, Dad worked from 7.30 am till 1 pm on a Saturday, and always left for work with the instructions, 'Now, don't get on your mother's nerves.'

This was a challenge that was solved by keeping out of the house as much as possible. Once I was deemed old enough I used to take Colin to the pictures in nearby Colchester on the bus. This was when I was about eleven years old and he was nine. Not that I always took him to suitable films. Restrictions were lighter then and Saturday morning children's films included many that would now be rated for twelve-year olds or above. I still remember the last scene from Jason and the Golden Fleece, when the sailors are sword-fighting and skeletons, skulls and bones are flying everywhere. I loved it, but I turned to see Colin had slid down under his seat with his eyes closed! The bus journey home was spent with me begging him not to tell Mum I had taken him to a scary film. He didn't tell. Once we were older, we spent more and more time at the stables, riding, mucking out and grooming our horses, and those of others. Home became somewhere from which we both tried to escape at every possible opportunity.

In Colin's final days, a student nurse at the hospital took an interest in him as he lay unconscious. 'Was there any particular trauma that made him like this?' she asked, sliding her eyes towards his inert shape, and comparing it with a photo that I had brought to the hospital. I had stood this on the cabinet by his bed, to remind those caring for him of who he was. It showed Colin four years earlier, standing beside me and laughing while on his first Portuguese holiday.

I thought hard, but couldn't come up with any identifiable cause, though I recognized that Colin had suffered on and off from depression for many years. I only knew that because he confided in me after a sympathetic doctor had taken time to talk to him about his various dependencies. Of course, then prescribing him anti-depressants may not have been the best answer for someone already addicted to Class A drugs!

Colin once said that it was all very tiring, frustrating, depressing and guilt-inducing and he sometimes didn't know where his addiction ended and his depression started. He felt that life stresses were the problem and the alcohol and drugs were the solution. They made him less depressed, at least temporarily. But of course, they very quickly became the problem and contributed to wild mood swings, moments of absence and other times when he was as twitchy as a puppet on a string.

We always want to be able to pin someone's behaviour on something that could have been avoided had

15

we known about it early enough. We'd all like to be able to blame our parents for our later troubles. But many children in the 1950s were born to uncommunicative parents who concentrated on overcoming the economic poverty of the 1940s and raising physically healthy children on 'Delrosa' rosehip syrup, school-provided milk and cod liver oil.

In early 1958 when Colin was nearly two years old our mother suffered a 'nervous breakdown' and went into a mental hospital in London, to be treated with electro-convulsive therapy (ECT). Nowadays I am sure this would have been identified as the culmination of her enduring post-natal depression after his birth, and she would have received more sympathetic treatment. As it is even now, ECT was a popular and supposedly successful treatment for unhappy women in the 1950s but she came back to us after several months with gaps in her memory and still suffering terrible bouts of depression. As mentioned earlier, her own addiction to Valium when it was made available in the 1960s helped to alleviate some of her despair and sometimes downright paranoia, but we still spent a lot of time tiptoeing around her moods.

While Mum was away in hospital and immediately after her return, Colin went lived with a kind auntie. This lasted for nearly a year. She was our mother's cousin and would have liked to keep Colin with her in an informal family fostering arrangement, but my parents wanted him back, which is understandable. The ECT had supposedly 'cured' Mum, and they were going to buy a house on the coast nearer to her mother and father and all would be well. Unfortunately, living next door to her own parents led to arguments and fights and long periods when they were not talking to each other, adding to the turmoil at home. This worsened after the death a few years later of our peace-keeping grandfather.

On reflection, maybe our auntie should have kept Colin. His older male cousins might have been a good influence and who knows, he may have grown up to be a very different person? Talking to one of those cousins after Colin's funeral, we shared memories of what a dear little boy he was, and how things could have been.

Summer 1959

There is a school of thought that views alcohol and drug addiction as 'ritualised compulsive comfort-seeking' in the face of adverse childhood experiences (ACEs). I can see the sense in that. My brother and I comforted each other as children, as I made excuses for him to Dad and he tried to explain to me how to manage Mum's anger: 'No need to argue every point; just don't tell them what you're doing, and then there's no argument.' And this was how he proceeded for the rest of their lives. For those interested in reading more about ACEs as a possible reason for addiction, you can go to acestoohigh.com for more information.

However, whatever the reasons for anyone's addiction, what is needed are some practical ideas of how to help and how to stay in contact with them.. A lot of time can be wasted on reproaching ourselves for not noticing what was happening, and not preventing future dependence and illness. Don't blame yourself. Just make a decision on how much you can help and do it.

You may be reading this book after you have given up on your relative and broken all contact. Eventually far more relatives and friends rejected Colin than kept in touch with him. But the sadness in their faces at his funeral, and conversations held with them over the years impressed upon me that, although we may all deal with a loved one's addiction in different ways, deal with it we must. Breaking off contact with someone is still traumatic, requiring shutting down reactions, turning away, repressing thoughts. The feelings will surface from time to time and will need to be pushed down again. We have to deal with them, whether it is by sticking with our loved one or turning away. They are always there.

CHAPTER TWO

AS A FATHER

Try not to judge what you cannot know

Colin fathered two sons but was only a father in any true sense to one of them. Rickie was born in the late 1970s to a previous girlfriend and they split up when he was under a year old. She married a few years later, her husband adopted the little boy as his own and none of us had any further contact. He would be over forty years old now. Colin mentioned once that he knew where Rickie worked, and that he had gone to the grammar school and 'done well' for himself, but I was never sure if that was true or not.

In the mid-1980s, Colin married Ginny and they had Steven shortly afterwards. I didn't receive an invitation to the wedding, and nor did Mum and Dad, but Colin sneaked a couple of wedding photos to our mother and later gave her one of Steven as a baby. By then our father was no longer talking to him and would not even acknowledge his existence. Only recently did I understand how very hurtful that was, and also how difficult it made life for Mum.

I was pleased for Colin and Ginny and visited them in their council flat home. While it was clear that Colin, twitching away, was definitely 'on something', we managed to keep friendly contact so long as I avoided the subject. He was in and out of work, but they seemed to be happy. Then, suddenly, Ginny did not return from a Spanish holiday with her best friend, and Colin was left on his own with his three-year-old son to look after. Evidently she was also on drugs, and not just amphetamines, and the drug scene in Barcelona was just too tempting. She sent Steven back with her friend, and Colin was contacted to come and collect him from the airport. I guess my perception of their happiness may have been somewhat inaccurate! He was devastated but managed to hold it all together somehow and was determined not to lose Steven, whom he loved fiercely.

His biggest fear was that the social services would get wind of the fact that he, an addict, was raising a little boy alone on one of the roughest council estates. He tried to find a different location in which to live. Eventually they moved to a council flat in a better area, and Steven was enrolled in a local primary school.

Something I am sure family members of those with addiction problems recognise, is the continual struggle in your own mind to separate the person from the addiction. Colin, the person of my childhood memories, became more visible while his son was young: he dug the large garden at the back of his council flat and planted potatoes, peas, beans and strawberries; he played football with Steven and bought him clothes and toys from the local charity shop. While he was certainly not off the drink and drugs, they seemed a smaller part of his life. Steven was a quiet, polite boy who was doing well at school, and Colin attended every parents' evening and reported back to me with pride.

Young gardeners in Autumn 1957

It was as if he took the best parts of our childhood and tried to give them to Steven. Our father was a keen gardener who looked after his own large garden and that of our paternal grandparents, and there are several pictures of Colin and me as little more than toddlers with small forks and wheelbarrows. Colin continued to love gardening, as do I, and until a few years ago he would cycle miles to do other people's gardens for them, often for very little payment.

Dad met regularly with teachers to discuss our progress at school, and bought us books and comics, while Mum took us to the library as small children. Books were always part of our growing up, and Colin ensured they were also part of Steven's. They had a strong father-son bond in Steven's early childhood.

But Colin was also lonely for other adult company, and of course that meant the company of those who would share beer, fags and drugs. Gradually the flat became more rundown-looking and I was aware of unfamiliar friends who left as soon as I arrived. The video player I bought him one Christmas disappeared within weeks ('Stolen', Colin shrugged) and a hole was smashed in his front door as those to whom he owed drug money tried to collect on the debts.

Occasionally Colin had bruises, and I suspected that the dealers had caught up with him. It was a dark world that I wanted no part of, and he would lie freely to me to keep me out of it. But the feeling that my brother was in danger curdled my stomach.

Despite this Steven seemed to be thriving, though he was a shy boy, and I worried about him. Colin had several female friends with children who occasionally had Steven over to stay at night in the school holidays. And he seemed to have a little group of school friends, with whom he played football outside, though I noticed they never seemed to come to play indoors, despite the large table football in his bedroom.

In retrospect, I wasn't nearly involved enough with Colin at this stage, but I had my own three sons to look after, and my first husband was not at all sympathetic to my brother's ways, so visiting him wasn't easy. Why didn't I do more to support him with childcare? Well, Steven certainly wasn't comfortable enough with me to come over to ours. He was nearly ten years younger than my children and there was nothing in common. But I think the true reason is that I really wanted to believe that we were still looking at a bit of cannabis or amphetamines occasionally, and too many beers. Not heroin or cocaine. Though the evidence was there to see, in Colin's hyperactivity interspersed with daytime sleepiness. But my expertise regarding symptoms of opioid addiction came a lot later. Twenty-five years ago, I was still an innocent.

Visiting became easier as my children grew older and I qualified as a teacher and was out and about more. I taught locally and could add in a quick visit to Colin on my way home some nights. I became ever more worried as any items of value seemed to be disappearing from his flat. It was a moment of wry humour that our mother left me her bent old knitting needles in her will and bequeathed to Colin her antique treadle sewing machine that with its beautifully kept walnut cabinet and shiny oiled machinery was certainly 'worth a bob or two', as Colin commented. He stored it just inside his door for a while, and then that too disappeared. Her death was very hard on him, as she had maintained contact behind our father's back over the years, and he now seemed like nobody's son. Dad still ignored his existence, filled with shame over his rough-looking offspring, who was clearly not the adult son he had hoped for.

I hadn't realised how very much our father's rejection of him hurt Colin till he mentioned that a few months before Dad died in 1997, he had tried to visit him in the nursing home. By then our father was in a wheelchair as he had lost a leg due to diabetes, but on seeing Colin, he turned his chair to the wall and refused to look at him till my brother went away again. Soon after Dad passed away Colin spoke to me about this and declared through tears that he would be a much better father to his son than our father had been to him. I know he tried to be, but the fact that Steven had nothing to do with him once he in turn fathered his own children tells a different story.

I sometimes tried to ask Colin what he was on, and if he couldn't get off it. This usually led to a swift change of subject or an abrupt end to the phone conversation as hung up on me. He admitted some years ago in a letter that he later asked me to destroy, that he had been injecting heroin since he was twenty-one but was by then, at forty, 'only on methadone.' I remember this methadone interlude as a relatively calm period when Steven was in the early years of secondary school, but unfortunately it didn't last long. Then the Colin that I knew and loved began to withdraw again.

He seemed to be out a lot when I visited, though one hot summer's day I found him fast asleep on his back in the garden, a chocolate digestive melting gently into his chest! He laughed and tried unsuccessfully to lick off the sticky goo when I woke him up. Daytime sleeping and nocturnal dealing when Steven was (hopefully) safely in bed became an established pattern of which I was only aware when I looked back on events, though I would have been helpless to change it anyway.

And that is maybe one secret of how to cope and not break the contact. You have to accept what you can't change. I couldn't engage Colin in conversation about his habits, because the shutters would come down. We always said that we loved each other, and I know that was true for him as well as me. He tried to protect me from the truth and the worst threat (in his mind) that any friend could give was, 'I'll tell your sister what you're up to.'

Sometimes in the later years there would be phone calls from girlfriends to me, living many miles away in Portugal.

'He's smoking crack again…he's injecting again…he keeps falling and passing out…he begged me not to tell you…he doesn't know I'm ringing you…please don't tell him…he took my card and got more money out. I don't know what to do.'

They were all depressingly similar. All somehow seemed to think I would be able to help. I would say that I knew, and that they should protect themselves and their bank card. After they rang off, still declaring that they 'loved him to bits' - goodness knows why they did- I would cry.

But these calls didn't come during Steven's childhood. They were safely in their council flat and, somehow, Colin was fulfilling the father role while still drinking and dealing and taking drugs. I could not prove this of course, but I could see it in his increasing twitchiness, and I could hear the mad dash to clear away visible evidence when I knocked on his door. Bin bags full of cans began to replace the plants on the balcony, and the previously cultivated garden grew over with weeds.

However, as is the case with life, things were not all bad all of the time. While Steven was a young boy, holidays were spent with Colin's friend Hayley and her son Will in their old camper van, travelling in Cornwall and Devon. Will and Steven got on well, and - at least to hear Colin reminisce - those were magical times. Once Steven was a teenager, he became more and more uncommunicative with his 'Auntie Laura' and I really did not know what was going on in his mind. He would say hello politely and then leave the flat. Colin would shrug and say, 'What can you do?' But, although I was sure Steven smoked and drank beer with his mates, there was never any sign of him taking drugs, so I kept my fingers crossed. Their flat was on a large estate, and there were many social problems, with easy access to substances, had he wanted to take them. Maybe his Dad served as a warning that protected him.

The crunch in their relationship seemed to come when Colin's steady girlfriend moved into the flat. From having his father to himself, Steven was now sharing him with another. Michelle was also an alcoholic and on methadone. She said she wasn't taking any other drugs, but her tipple was vodka, rather than the strong beer that Colin favoured. Colin had always been - I think - a reasonably placid drunk; Michelle was anything but. Steven didn't seem to like her, and nor did many of Colin's friends. The relationship was quite turbulent, and a crisis came with Colin's eviction from the flat. He had hidden from me the fact he was in rent arrears, and while Steven was under 18 and dependent on his father, the council would not evict him. But a few weeks after Steven's 18th birthday, the eviction notice came, and the bailiffs sealed the door. Colin was enraged. How dare they? Winter was coming and Michelle and he were homeless. Steven, luckily for him, was already living with his girlfriend's parents.

Colin rang me, but the best I could do was send him details of possible local places to rent that I found on the internet and promise to pay the first few weeks for them. They found somewhere after several weeks of moving from friend to friend and hostel to hostel. Colin was incensed by the fact that the hostels didn't allow alcohol on the premises (even beer hidden in a Lucozade bottle!) So, he preferred to wear out his welcome with friends. It was this unrealistic attitude and refusal to face up to any problems that characterised Colin. The private places they were renting were more than their combined housing benefit, and I started ordering food deliveries from Tesco's for them, at first sporadically and then regularly. When Colin had no fixed home, I sent the food to Steven's address and asked him to meet his Dad somewhere and hand it over. It upset me to hear over the phone how unwilling he was to do this, and I realised how conflicted he felt about his father.

Finally, Colin and Michelle moved into a permanent bedsit on the outskirts of town, part of a terraced block run by a landlord happy to be the direct recipient of housing benefit in exchange for housing those on social security. It was tiny, but contained a washing machine and cooker, and a shower room with toilet. It was a lot smaller than the flat from which he had been evicted, but they seemed happy enough there. Meanwhile, Steven and his girlfriend Karen had also found somewhere of their own, and Colin's first grandson was born in December 2008. I still remember the call from Colin - he was ecstatic and used all his phone credit before I could call him back. Taken back to Steven's early years, he was determined to be a good granddad to this little one and started immediately collecting baby clothes and toys from charity shops.

But the contact was very brief. Steven stopped answering his Dad's phone calls and began to withdraw even further from him. Colin blamed Karen for this, but I feel that Steven was looking to make his life without his father in order to protect his young family, and himself. He would talk to him if they met accidentally, and when Colin found out where he was working he would sometimes wait for him at the end of the day, but truly it was a heart-breaking situation. A second grandson was born in 2012. Two years after that Colin threw away the toys, after holding onto them in hope for six years. I gave him a few photos of his grandchildren that I had found on Facebook -

one the absolute image of Colin himself as a child - and he framed and displayed them, as wholly inadequate replacements for the real thing.

This situation also hurt me deeply. By the time our father died in 1997 not only was he not talking to Colin, his only son, but neither did he have contact with his two surviving brothers; our mother's split from her own mother and her brother had caused a lot of heartbreak; our parents' rejection of me when I had lived with my first husband before we were married was only partly healed by the arrival of their first grandson. I realise now that we came from a deeply divided and rejecting family. Our response had been to cling closely together as children, and to try to keep this closeness, against all the odds sometimes, as adults. It seemed Steven was recreating rifts, though another part of me totally understood this need to protect himself and his young family. Colin had some contact with my own children and grandchildren but being an uncle to mine was a poor substitute for being a dad and granddad to his own.

In mid-2018, I resolved to try and do something about this. I tracked down Steven's partner, by now his wife, on Facebook, and also found their home address through the local library and electoral roll. I wrote to them, enclosing photos, Colin's phone number and his address. By now he was living alone in his supported housing, and I hoped this would mean that Steven felt able to visit, even if he didn't want to bring the children. The only reply was a brief note on Facebook from Karen thanking me for the photos and letter and promising to pass on all the details to

Steven. Nothing else, and I never told Colin about this, because there was nothing to be gained by it, only more hurt feelings.

As Colin's health deteriorated through 2018 and into 2019, I sent several Facebook messages to Karen. Did Steven want to visit his Dad? Here, again, was the address and phone number. He didn't visit, though she responded in a friendly enough manner. My attempts to get them together before Colin died had clearly failed.

When I messaged Karen and Steven with the news of Colin's death, they wanted to know about the cremation details. I sent them and held my breath again. I was so happy to see them both at the funeral, and Steven was visibly upset at the loss again of the father he had lost for the first time so many years ago. We are still in regular communication as the rifts are healing. It is wonderful for me to have contact with my nephew and his family and I am determined to see as much of them as is possible over the coming years. Something good has to come from Colin's absence, and this is it.

Even the most incorrigible addict needs to know that their family loves them. Colin knew he always had me. Not to see his son and grandsons hurt him just as much as it would hurt a non-addict. Young children can be taught by example and to have a grandfather or uncle who is clearly so dependent on health-wrecking substances is one of the best life lessons that can be learnt. My own grandchildren saw Colin occasionally, and my two sons who lived in the same town as he did also kept in sporadic contact with their Uncle Colin. But I cannot blame Steven for rejecting his father. I have never been the child of an addict and dealer. Maybe that is a special kind of hurt that only those suffering it can understand. Steven's eyes at the funeral said it all. His life both with and without his father's presence had been very hard, and no decision is without pain.

CHAPTER THREE

AS A BROTHER

It's OK to be angry sometimes

As a young boy, Colin was a loyal brother, and a lot of fun. Though his lack of responsibility (perhaps because he was always seen as my responsibility) often meant trouble for me. More than once a game of hide and seek in the woods ended with my cycling home in a panic as I couldn't find him, only to find he was there already and laughing at me through the window. I eventually got wise and refused to play.

During the school holidays, once we had done the shopping on our bikes we were free to roam around and we got on well together, despite being so different in many ways. The mischief we got up to was fairly harmless: things like lying quietly in the long grass on overgrown graves the cemetery behind our home and jumping up screaming as people walked past, playing on rotten old houseboats and entering derelict houses looking for treasure or ghosts. We had a healthy fear of adults who would bang on windows and shout at us as we crept through their gardens playing 'Indians' and would cycle miles in a day, returning for tea just before it got dark.

Once we were teenagers we still never 'told' on each other and conspired to protect ourselves from parental wrath. I missed Colin when I left home, and once he realised that our mother, in her anger at my first husband and I living 'in sin' before we married, was intent on destroying all my possessions, he managed to save some of my books and photos and bring them to me, smuggling them out of the house inside his leather jacket. Looking back now, I can see how much he cared.

When our mother was dying in 1991, I needed some relief from sitting at her hospital bedside for four days and I hoped Colin would share this time with me. I rang and asked him to come to the hospital. He walked in, became visibly upset, and left again. That was that. His final visit to Mum lasted all of three minutes. His response to stress was always avoidance. I helped our father and our uncle organise the funeral, the flowers and the donations, and Colin turned up late, as he had been stopped by the police on the way for driving a friend's car that was untaxed and for which he was not insured. Typically, he hadn't thought to allow enough time to catch the bus and had scrounged a car to dash to his mother's funeral. I would often feel frustration at his lack of forethought; this time I was angry and had difficulty even being polite to him. Of course, I hadn't thought to organise a lift for him, had I?

Luckily for both of us, before I could vent my anger, he had to leave again straight after the service - possibly sensing that this time he had overstepped some mark, or maybe unable to face the graveside. Over the years, while he may have visited our parents' grave occasionally, so far as I know he never placed flowers nor pulled up so much as a weed. Colin was cremated and so will I be. Just memories and a scattering of ashes - no graves to add yet another layer of guilt for surviving relatives.

I have looked back over this paragraph and it sounds unkind, but that's how it was sometimes. I didn't always feel compassionate towards Colin, though I hope he didn't recognise it. If you are reading this book because you have a dear relative or close friend who is an addict, I am sure you can identify with these feelings of impatience, frustration and downright anger.

I don't remember Colin coming to our father's funeral, though he may have done. However, by then they were totally estranged. Paying for nursing home care had depleted our father's savings and he left me a small amount in his will. I told Colin he had left him some money too, although he hadn't, and gave him £1000, which was exactly half our Dad's inheritance. He was thrilled and bought a large motorbike, but then never managed to tax and insure it and it stood in his garden until it was sold, a useless testament to his dreams. But for Colin the best gift was the thought that his Dad had loved him enough to leave him something.

In 1994 I left my first marriage after twenty-one years, but Colin was one of the last to know. I figured he had enough problems, and I turned to friends for my support. Although I needed somewhere to stay for a few months, he was not the obvious choice! I do know the few times I had asked Colin's help for anything, he was always willing, but he had difficulty in following through. For example, as he was on personal independence payments (PIP), because of reduced mobility due to his failing lungs, he was entitled to a free bus pass. I was planning a very quick visit one time and said that I would get the forms and fill them out as best I could, and then all that would be needed was his signature. To help me out, could he get his photos taken in one of the booths in town? I sent £5 in a letter, and hoped he'd be ready to go and get his pass. Naïve of me. When I arrived with the papers all completed and asked where the photos were, he admitted the £5 had gone across the bar. So, we went to the photo booth together!

Colin was late every time I met up with him, was useless at ever retrieving any property he had pawned for quick cash and missed most of his medical appointments unless I managed to ring him early enough on the same morning to remind him. He did care, but just wasn't able to be organised enough to follow through.

However, when my husband, Uwe, was seriously ill in hospital over 10 years ago, Colin was really concerned, and asked regularly how he was. He was amazed how well he recovered, marvelling, 'He's fifteen years older than me, and look at him!'

Yes, well, what could I say? Uwe doesn't have a drug and alcohol problem. Colin's care for others continued right to the end. He spent time shopping for others who couldn't get out, though it had to be tiny amounts, as physically his COPD was limiting the distance he could walk with even a small bag of groceries. I was always thanked for coming over to visit, for taking him out, for the holidays, the chat, the quick drink together, or the meal. He always asked after my three sons and the grandchildren if he hadn't seen them lately. 'How are the boys and the kids?' was his first question when I visited, although the 'boys' were then in their forties and most of the grandchildren were teenagers!

About seven years ago, Michelle inherited her father's house near Wales and had a lot of money at a point when I was struggling to help another family member pay off some debts, and they kindly offered to help out with a loan. I accepted - until I realised that Colin kept taking Michelle's bank card to draw out cash that never reached me. I scraped together the money myself.

Nonetheless, that Christmas, in an effort to make up for what he viewed as his lapses as an uncle, he sent each of my sons £50 in a card with an apology and instructions to 'enjoy yourself.' They were really touched, and we shared a few tears over this. Sending this money was quite a feat for someone who normally couldn't keep a pound coin for more than a few moments. However, having easy access to money, whoever's it was, always added to Colin's drink and drug problems. The relationship with Michelle foundered on her inheritance, or to be more accurate, her dismay at the speed with which he was going through it. He returned to Essex alone, ostensibly to get away from the dealers and drug scene in Bristol, but really because she had thrown him out and he had nowhere else to go.

Colin always tried to hide the worst of his habits from me. Whenever I visited, ashtrays were emptied, and cans swept away and I was offered a coffee. I helped him in this by phoning before I called round. I was a bit earlier than expected one day and found Colin smoking in the back yard behind the bedsit while his latest loyal partner Denise, who was with him to the end, was pushing a large old vacuum cleaner in ever-decreasing circles around the tiny space of uncluttered carpet in an effort to 'clean up'.

'Hoover's too big for this place,' she commented, giving up and flopping back on the unmade bed.

Our times together were not without humour. As we walked slowly down the street one day, and people parted for us, as usually happened once they saw Colin's somewhat dishevelled appearance, he turned to me and grinned. 'Like Moses parting the Red Sea,' he quipped, and we both fell about laughing.

Another time I was hugging Colin goodbye in the town centre, and he pulled back from me and said, 'Watch it - people will think you're getting a bit friendly for a social worker!' Ha! He knew me well. In my smartish trousers and sensible flat shoes I looked every inch the professional carer. I watched him amble away to join his street drinker mates on the bench, each with their strong beer tipped into a Lucozade or iced tea bottle or slipped inside a brown paper bag, fooling nobody. They knew every CCTV camera in the town and were adept at avoiding them. Sometimes Colin and I would be walking from the Citizen's Advice bureau or the shops back to his place, and he would pull me into a side street with a convenient wall on which he could sit while having a swig of his 'Lucozade.'

'No cameras here', he'd reassure me, as I settled on the wall beside him. However, as time passed and Colin went from being energetic and wiry to skeletal and shambling, I began to fear that each goodbye might be the last one. I said as much a few weeks before he died. He looked up at me from the armchair in which he was sitting hunched over in Denise's lavender-coloured dressing gown and gave a gurgling, chesty laugh, 'Ever optimistic - aren't you the cheerful one?'

One of the funniest stories was when Colin decided to walk round to my oldest son's house. He really liked his nephews and loved to play with their children. However, he had become side-tracked as he passed a couple of pubs on the way, and it was midnight before he covered the two miles between his place and my son's. Realising it was too late to visit, and not wanting to wake the children, he knocked at the neighbour's door.

'Got a pen and a bit of paper, please? I want to put a note through next door, as I'm a bit too late to visit now.'

The neighbour obliged, and my son woke up to an illegibly scribbled note on the doormat and an irate neighbour whose whole family had been roused by my brother. This illustrates perfectly the slightly 'off' thinking that characterised Colin as the years of addiction took their toll.

Sometimes I would see him through other people's eyes, and it would bring me up short, as I realized how he appeared. One day in the late 1990s before I emigrated to teach overseas, I left the local college about 5 pm and came across Colin sitting on the edge of the pavement with some friends and a few cans. I stopped to have a chat. It was unusual for me to bump into him on the street, and at first I wondered if he'd positioned himself there to catch me and ask for money, which he should have known I wouldn't give. Maybe the friends were for backup? But my suspicions proved unfounded, as I was introduced cordially as 'my sister', and there were pleasant nods all round. I gave him the usual hug, and promised to visit the next week, waving goodbye as I walked away. A young teacher from my department ran to catch up with me. 'Someone you know?' she asked curiously. 'My brother.' I replied. Conversation stopper.

I needed a sense of the absurd in order not to weep at the lack of logic in the way Colin lived. Or at least there was a different logic in the way he lived. Of course, this was provoked by the need to always somehow have enough money for the next can or smoke, even if that meant going without food, missing a couple of payments on the TV licence, or running the pound coins through the electricity meter a couple of times. Or picking up cigarette butts on the street, to my huge consternation when we were walking together one day! Yet he loved to browse in charity shops and buy knick-knacks for a pound or two, to arrange along the already cluttered shelves at home. So, he would collect things instead of paying bills or buying food. And this was before I had begun to step in, so there was the real possibility that the small china cup and saucer or chipped vase meant no meal that night. Of course, the pub would always put a few beers on 'tick' for him. He never went without drink.

Uwe and I had a register office wedding in 2008, attended by Colin, of course. He cleaned up well, and really enjoyed the day. A friend snapped a picture of us having a good laugh together after the ceremony. It captures Colin perfectly.

At our wedding in 2008

I think it was our closeness in our earlier years that helped me stick by Colin and try and help him later. Once I realised that his drinking and drug-taking was not a teenage phase, I didn't want to make excuses for him as our mother had, nor to reject him like our father. I tried a middle path of supporting but not enabling, but apart from letting him know that through it all there was at least one person who loved him, I failed at this. If I hadn't, he would still be alive.

But all friends and relatives have to be prepared to fail if our aim is to get our loved one off the drugs and alcohol. You can buy their food, even pay rent, council tax and TV licence, visit and talk and tell them you love them. However, you cannot keep them alive through your willpower. It takes their willpower. And from what I could see, this varied considerably in my brother. Holidays with us were where he showed the greatest resistance, and at home with his friends where he showed the least.

CHAPTER FOUR

HOLIDAYS

A change of scenery brings out the best in everyone

As I mentioned earlier, Colin used to go away in a camper van with his friend Hayley when Steven was little. But apart from that he had never really had a holiday. When I married for the second time in 2008, Uwe and I settled in Portugal. This geographical distance from Colin allowed some emotional distance as well. When he seemed to be going through a better patch in 2015 (taking prescribed methadone rather than buying heroin) we encouraged him to visit on an all-expenses paid holiday. My friends told me I'd be pleased that, finally, I had invited Colin to come and stay, but I was very nervous. I wondered if I could trust him not to bring drugs. I wondered how he would manage without the 8% special brew he was used to, which was not for sale in our little seaside town. I wondered if we should buy him a new suitcase - one that hadn't had cannabis smoked over it, nor been used to store goodness knows what.

I needn't have feared. We bought the suitcase; he drank our bottles of 'Coral' beer a crate at a time and was clearly managing on the methadone tablets that he brought with him. Methadone is normally prescribed in liquid form, but that would have been impossible to pack. Bringing his tablets was one of the most complicated parts of planning the trip.. A doctor's letter was needed explaining the presence of a Class A drug in the hand luggage, with the exact numbers, date of prescription and destination of travel. But the STaRS drug and alcohol support unit jumped into action and helped out with all the tricky bits. In July 2015, Colin and I boarded the National Express coach for the airport. No alcohol was allowed on the bus, but the useful Lucozade bottle acted as a good cover, and every time there was a stop of more than a few minutes, Colin hopped off for a smoke. I hadn't thought before about the details of travelling with someone so dependent on these props.

The attention we received while travelling together was something it took me a while to get used to. Most fellow travellers were polite and kind, but when we asked the Gatwick airport staff where the smoking area was, and if there was a bar near the departure gate we received very abrupt answers. One black-suited woman wearing a security vest looked at Colin, bent and gasping and gave him a strong telling off, commenting that 'By the look of you, you should give up smoking and drinking, now.' Very helpful!

Going through security was also interesting. Colin, proud of his 'clean' status decided to boast about it. 'Nothing on me,' he declared loudly as we went through the checks. 'No gear, nothing. Look if you like.'

They liked. His backpack and all contents were taken away, including his inhalers, to be passed through several drug swabs. This brought on a fit of shaking and gasping so drastic that I thought maybe one of us wouldn't make it on holiday.

'Oi, where're you going? I need my things!'

Then, wheezing and coughing, Colin was asked to remove his belt and shoes, revealing his pitiful thinness as he clutched at his trousers with one hand, and bent to unlace his boots with the other. I was helpless, having passed through security ahead of him, and not allowed back to assist. Somebody found a chair, and he sat down, head bent and shoulders heaving, as those in the queue behind were waved through.

I sighed and squinted across at his bag. 'Can he at least have the brown inhaler back, please?'

A kind airport security guard saw the problem and ran across with it. Colin's nail file was confiscated, and he repacked. 'Need a drink after that,' he spluttered and we moved through to the waiting area near the departure gate, where he then unnerved our fellow passengers by asking them where the nearest place was for a 'swaller'. He patted them on the arm reassuringly, saying 'Don't mind me,' when they stared at him, uncomprehending. We set off to find the bar for his quick 'swaller' So far so good.

I took the middle seat on the plane to Lisbon, while Colin had the aisle. This enabled him to get up and down for the toilet and to stretch his legs as often as he liked, but when he choked on the soggy bread roll so beloved of the Portuguese airlines, I was trapped in my seat beside him and unable to do anything other than press the call bell. An energetic and highly efficient attendant came quickly up the aisle, undid the seatbelt and hauled Colin from his seat, subjecting him to a vigorous but successful Heimlich manoeuvre that brought up the roll and a fair quantity of beer into the central aisle. Other travellers turned their heads away and cast their eyes sideways at us.

'Bloody hurt my ribs that did!' Colin complained ungratefully. After signing the mandatory incident sheet, he wandered nonchalantly to the back of the plane, returning with two more cans of beer, to recover from his trauma. After his liquid lunch he dozed quietly and the rest of the journey was uneventful. We could relax in the sun for two weeks under the non-judgmental gaze of my Portuguese neighbours and he could gather his energy for the return trip.

Colin came to Portugal twice. The first holiday in 2015 was the most successful from all points of view, though it had a slightly disturbing start. Uwe met us at the tiny airport and we drove home in ten minutes. We showed Colin where he would be sleeping: a downstairs bedroom with direct access to the steps just inside the garden gate where he could sit and smoke at any time. It also had direct access to the kitchen, and a fridge with beer. All other alcohol had been locked away for the duration. Colin glanced around, declared the room 'great' and then said he wanted to go for a walk by himself before dinner. 'Just to explore the place.'

Uwe and I exchanged glances. We knew that he was probably trying to size up the nearest bar and also any local potential for drugs. It was only about 7 pm, so any bars - as well as being at least thirty minutes away on foot - would probably be closed or empty. The Portuguese begin their evenings out at 9 pm at the earliest. We provided him with a local card for his phone, and our phone numbers and off he went.

One hour passed, and another half an hour and it was getting dark. Then my phone rang. 'Not got a clue where I am, Laura,' Colin gasped. 'Standing near a big yellow recycling bin.' There are about twenty of those within a few miles of our house. Not much help.

'Can you see the sea?' I asked him. 'No, black as yer hat here,' came the reply.

'OK, walk downhill from wherever you are and you should arrive at the beach. We'll put all our lights on in the house and come in the car and find you. If you see a house lit up like a beacon, it's ours and you can ring me back.'

Unless he had walked a lot further than we felt possible, the chances were that we would find him quite quickly. We jumped in the car and drove slowly down towards the beach - and there he was, sitting on a low wall, looking thin and vulnerable, and very pleased to see us. Also, it seemed he had realised that we really lived 'out in the sticks' and nighttime walks would yield nothing more than a breath of fresh air. That was his first and last solitary nocturnal excursion.

Uwe took Colin on a 'plant tour' of our small garden. 'Ah, Brugmansia,' exclaimed Colin knowledgeably, looking at our angel's trumpet tree. Uwe was very impressed, but less so when I said that Colin had probably known the name because all parts of this tree have hallucinogenic properties. It is more than an ornamental bush. Hence his excellent gardening knowledge!

Colin was reasonably well during this fortnight, though the texts that continued to ping into his phone made me realise that he could not be completely 'clean', else why were the dealers pursuing him so relentlessly? It touched me to think that he was brave enough to take the step of removing himself from all of his support to come on holiday. And we had a good holiday: horse-riding, walking a little, visiting the beach, sleeping in the sun, eating out, a barbecue at ours where he chatted and laughed with our friends about football. I cried when I saw him onto the plane back to England. Why hadn't I done this before?

I still have the letter Colin wrote me before this first holiday, thanking me for inviting him and promising not to 'let me down.' That last phrase still makes me feel guilty: was I so judgemental of him that he always had to pretend, and try to be something he wasn't? The sad truth is - probably, yes. And I think several people reading this will understand. Maybe you have asked yourselves how your intelligent young relative or friend with everything in front of them could become so addicted to alcohol and drugs that they could no longer live any sort of normal life? Colin was bright and lively. He would sit in front of TV quiz shows and answer all the questions. He loved Mastermind and University Challenge, although admittedly neither of us could answer all the questions on those! He had many friends, though during the later years more and more of them were addicts, as others had less to do with him.

Portugal 2015

I invited him back to Portugal the next year, and this time took the aisle seat across from him on the plane, just in case he attempted to eat the roll again! But all went well, except that our flight was delayed by several hours, which meant several more airport beers, and Colin wandered between the bar and the toilets, while I tried not to lose him. He then slept, snoring noisily, for most of the flight.

Portugal 2015

However, he was less well during this break. The methadone tablets seemed to be giving him stomach cramps, and several planned outings had to be cancelled. I have since learnt from others that he was back on crack cocaine by 2016 and probably going through some withdrawal as well. Doubly brave to come in that case. We went dolphin watching and he enjoyed that, though the bumpy ride out across the waves was almost more than his skeletal frame could tolerate. We rode horses again, this time ambling instead of cantering. We sat in the garden in the evening and chatted. My husband Uwe had grown fond of Colin, and they would have long conversations about this and that over their beers.

I am a light sleeper, and I heard Colin stir with a groan every night in his downstairs bedroom and go outside and sit on the steps by our gate for a cigarette, sometimes well into the early hours. He was becoming nocturnal again, and I knew that this was probably the last time he would be well enough to come out to Portugal. I turned over in bed and sighed.

My fears were confirmed when I rang Colin after he arrived back home. Evidently his legs had swelled badly on the return flight, even though it was only a few hours, and the coach from London back to the Essex coast had made things even worse. He'd had to get a taxi from the coach station to his flat and was now lying in bed with his legs raised as high as possible and feeling very ill. It took a week for the fluid to drain gradually, and as his circulation grew worse, periodic swelling of his legs became more and more of a problem.

Our last holiday together was when Uwe, Colin and I rented a cottage on Dartmoor in September 2017. The drive from Essex to the holiday home was long. Colin needed to stop for a drink and smoke at least every hour, so I made the most of this chance to stretch my legs, but it meant we arrived after dark. I had chosen the location carefully, so it was not within walking distance of any pubs, as I wanted to see Colin and spend some time with him without having to sit in bars all day to do it. It was all on one level, as he was not managing stairs because of a lack of breath. His bedroom had a bathroom just next to it, and ours had an ensuite shower and toilet, so all was well. We explored and went horse riding again - this time over the moors. As well as eating out, we took gentle walks along the beach, beside hedgerows and fields and explored small villages, often (unsurprisingly) ending up in a pub somewhere.

We entered a small pub restaurant one evening and looked at the menu. Colin asked which of the meals would be easy to chew. The barman hesitated, and Colin supplied, 'I'm feeling a bit under the weather.'

The young man wasn't very familiar with this phrase and looked puzzled. 'Well,' responded Colin, with a twinkle in his eye, 'it's better than saying I have a terminal illness and don't want to choke to death here in your pub, isn't it?'

The barman lowered his eyebrows and squinted at my brother, quickly suggesting the stew, and Colin went for it. He had none of his own teeth and managed with a top set of very old dentures, much repaired with superglue. But if he didn't chew, suck or mash morsels of food well they would get stuck in his oesophagus, leading to a lot of discomfort that was only resolved once Colin had made himself vomit.

But though it was tender the beef had fibres, and Colin chewed and sucked at length, and then delicately removed each piece from his mouth afterwards and arranged them neatly around the rim of his plate. My eyes widened, but not as wide as those of the couple on the table next to us. 'Great flavour,' he gurgled. I smiled.

Colin was an easy holiday companion, until it came to sleeping at night. By then my brother was quite deaf and almost completely nocturnal. He liked to watch television late into the early hours, with the volume on full. I was the driver for this holiday and needed to get more than two or three hours of sleep a night. Uwe is also hard of hearing, so he was totally unbothered by the noise coming from the living room. Besides the noise from the television, while Colin stood outside smoking he held loud midnight phone calls with Denise that would sometimes turn into arguments - goodness knows what about. At 4 am one morning, after lying awake for hours, I stormed into the living room of the cottage and demanded that the TV be turned off, and shouldn't he be in bed? Hurt and muttering to himself, he shuffled off and I lay awake feeling guilty.

Colin and Uwe at Spinster Rock, Devon

If I could change anything, I think it would be that there was too much secrecy between us. I wrote Colin a letter on impulse in early 2019, saying I knew he was back on drugs but Uwe and I still loved him and cared about him and wanted to take him out as much as we could. I wish now I had followed that up with real conversations, but it was hard. Usually, Denise was there when I saw him, but when we were alone in the car was when I had the chance. Why didn't I take it? I suppose it's because it might have ended up with me pleading for him to stop, or spoilt our relationship, and really by then I felt everything was hopeless. I just wanted to pretend it wasn't happening and have some happy times. I found the letter amongst his things after he died, ten months later. He had promised a reply, which never came, but at least he hadn't thrown away the note.

At Teignmouth 2017

Pretence does have some place in keeping yourself calm while trying to support your addicted relative. It allows you to engage with the person, talk about the news, football, neighbours, their pets, relationships and day to day trivia, rather than always being focused through the 'sickness' lens

CHAPTER FIVE

HIS BEST FRIEND

When stepping back is better than action

Animals can often take the place of friends and family. My brother always loved dogs. As small children we had a dog, but only for a very brief period of about a year. Unfortunately, poor Jenny was kept chained up in the backyard for hours at a time, as our mother couldn't cope with her liveliness in the house and had no idea how to train her. I really wonder why she stopped at the pet shop and bought the little puppy, though Colin and I were thrilled at the time. I could see from our father's reaction when he came home from work that evening that this had been an impulse buy. There was a lot of sighing and muttering, and Colin and I whispered fearfully that Jenny might not be allowed to stay. However, she was allowed to sleep in the kitchen that first night, and then Dad set to, demolishing an old chicken run to make a kennel for her. From then on she was banished outside.

Colin and I played with her continually, but at our young ages of about four and six years old knew no better than to run towards her teasingly, and then run away as she flew to the end of her chain barking wildly, to our mother's intense anger. I have felt so guilty about this ever since that I have always avoided any thought of owning a dog. Eventually, my brother got a nip on his finger as he waggled it at the end of Jenny's nose, and our father was prevailed upon to take the unfortunate animal to be 'put down', as our mother declared her to be vicious. It was several weeks before we understood the permanence of this. 'Put down where?' I wondered, speculating that Dad might have driven Jenny to the woods and let her go. We were inconsolable in our grief when we realized what it really meant.

Once he became an adult, my brother always swore he would have a dog and look after it properly, and to his credit he did. Several German Shepherd dogs beautifully trained by him, passed through his hands, the last, Spangles, being given to friends when he was homeless as he couldn't bear for her to be on the streets or sofa-surfing with him.

A few years ago, Colin was asked to house an elderly Jack Russell terrier unwanted by a previous owner, who returned the love lavished on him tenfold. The small dog's totally unsuitable name was Satan, and Colin promptly renamed him Fella. He was a good-tempered little animal who was happy to be walked to the pub at a very slow pace every day. I have always been sure that the same weight of depression that sat on our mother's shoulder was at least partly responsible for my brother's alcoholism and drug taking, and I know that when he didn't have a dog to care for he was immeasurably sadder.

Fella looking thoughtful

Luckily Denise also cared for Fella, and said he was the reason they both got up in the morning. She kindly looked after him when Colin joined us on holiday. This little dog had the power to get them both off the sofa and out of the flat; he made my brother laugh, and he was petted wherever they went, which meant that not all of Colin's contact with others when he was out and about was negative. With his arthritic limp, smiling mouth and a continually wagging tail, he attracted a lot of positive comments. Fella was later adopted by a friend of mine whose own Jack Russell terrier had died a while ago, and he outlived my brother by seven months to the day.

This got me thinking about the power of pet ownership. I am sure that those who are living on the streets are happy to have their dogs as protection, and maybe as an occasional aid to begging, but they are also friends. Dogs are non-judgmental company who, so long as they are fed and walked have a happy attitude towards life. They won't frown or purse their lips or avoid their owner's eyes when he's drunk or drugged. I realised how harsh people could be towards Colin and those like him, when I phoned him one day as he was walking. It was cold, and he was breathless, so I couldn't understand him.

I was about to tell him that I would ring back later, when I heard a furious male voice shout, 'Get away from my wall, you fucking druggie!'

Evidently, Colin had paused and leant against someone's garden wall to get his breath while trying to talk to me and had thus attracted the attention of the house owner. What a way to be spoken to. What a life! But when he had Fella with him, others' attention was focused on the 'dear little dog.'

I was grateful to the vets' surgery that allowed all bills for Fella's care to be sent to me and treated my brother with such kindness when he took the dog in for his check-ups and pain medication. One young vet commented to Colin regularly that Fella looked as if he was doing better than his owner! I was lucky to be able to pay food bills and vets' bills and make Colin and Fella's lives a little more comfortable. Seeing Colin sitting on a bench in the park as Fella and he debated who should go after the ball Colin had just thrown made me realise that, as dire as things seemed occasionally, all was not gloom.

In about 2014, Colin decided he could no longer tolerate his tiny cramped bedsit near the traffic lights on a busy road. He could never open his windows as the vehicle fumes made breathing even more difficult than it was already. I helped him complete an application for council housing in a one-person flat or sheltered accommodation. He had wanted me to fill in his request as a single person, so I did, and we discussed changing it later after Denise joined him, but Colin was adamant that he wanted to live alone.

It took another four years for his application to result in a warden controlled one-bedroomed flat in a much quieter cul-de-sac. His newly single status came as a bit of a shock to Denise, and she walked the mile from their previous shared home to stay overnight with Colin as often as she could. She thought this had been my doing, and Colin was inclined to allow her to believe this, as it made his life more peaceful. Kind of him! And typical of his tactics to avoid conflict.

The one thing the housing did not allow, however, was pets, and Fella had to stay with Denise. At first this had seemed to be no problem, but after a few months it became clear that Colin was the real dog lover, and Fella began to be seen as trouble. He was wetting on the floor and becoming fractious, and also putting on a lot of weight, as she fed him more often than she walked him.

Very soon after that Denise damaged both her wrists in a fall and was admitted to hospital several weeks after the accident, having been in denial that there was any lasting injury. She was very ill with sepsis, and Colin needed to take Fella. But of course, the sheltered housing supervisor soon realised that this was no temporary stay for the little dog and impressed upon my brother that he would be evicted if he didn't find somewhere else for his best friend to stay. I wrote to everyone I could think of, and luckily a friend whose own Jack Russell terrier had died a few months earlier stepped in. Fella had a new home.

There is a back story to this transfer of Fella that taught me a lesson about the fragility of my ability to solve Colin's problems. At the end of 2018, I was feeling quite pleased with myself: my brother was established in his little flat with a warden at the end of a red cord; Denise was taking care of Fella, and he was walked by one or other of them every day; Colin seemed to be managing financially. Hadn't we done well? Then Denise had her fall.

I went into activity overdrive, and e-mailed friends and relatives, attaching descriptions and pictures of the terrier looking appealing and mournful. Within two days I had the promise of a good home from the aforementioned friend. My brother and his dealer buddy promised to take Fella to his new abode on a certain evening the next week, and all was organised, or so I thought. But they missed the date, and the offer was withdrawn, as my friend who had been happy to take the dog felt she was being messed around, and this only boded disaster.

'I can't risk taking him and getting attached, and then have your brother turning up after a time wanting him back,' she told me. 'And anyway, Colin doesn't seem half as anxious as you are to re-house Fella.'

Of course, Colin wasn't anxious to let go of his precious dog. He never really had a sense of impending doom until it was too late. He was the person who had assured me years ago that he didn't owe much rent, and then rang me from a phone box to say that bailiffs had been, and the locks had been changed! He would not be anxious until he received an eviction notice and by then it would be too late.

I assured her I would let Colin know. I was distraught and wailed to my husband about the stupidity of my brother and how he only had himself to blame for his situation, and how useless it was to help him and how I wouldn't ever try again. Then I realised that a lot of this frustration and disappointment was about me, and not him. For once I hadn't been able to affect the situation, in my 'older, more capable sister' role. There is a lot of guilt in having a younger brother - or indeed anyone in the family - who is an addict and hitting problems.

'How could I have prevented this? How will I feel when he is on the streets with the dog?' I struggled with my feelings.

Then I sat back and did nothing. Living overseas had one advantage. It put geographical and emotional distance between me and my brother's problems and removed me from immediate action. Thinking about the situation, I was sure that my brother would turn up the next day with the dog, oblivious to the anxiety that he had caused, and that my friend would be moved to take Fella once she saw him. And so it transpired. I learnt a lesson about the limitations of my control and knew that one day the ultimate challenge would come and I would not be able to control anything anymore.

I have wondered since then if things might have been better if Colin had withdrawn his request for a nicer flat and stayed with Denise in their tiny bedsit, despite the car and bus fumes that made him so breathless. He complained regularly that the cramped conditions drove them both crazy, but it seems it drove Colin crazy more than Denise, who pursued him quite tirelessly once he moved out. Neither of them seemed to do so well without the other, despite their bickering. Losing his dog, and then spending large parts of his day alone seemed to be the beginning of a very steep downward slope for Colin. But I am just (as usual) being wise long after the event.

So, I don't begrudge street dwellers their dogs, and pets should be allowed in all social housing. Sometimes a dog or cat is the friend to care when others don't, and the warmth against a cold reality. If your addicted relative has a cat or a dog that they love, then supporting them in keeping the animal looked after is a useful way to help, if you can.

CHAPTER SIX

MONEY, MONEY, MONEY

Don't give cash directly, no matter how tempted

Managing finances was another difficult area. If payments weren't automatically deducted from Colin's benefit then they just as automatically became a problem. Government financial cutbacks have led to diminishing funds for local councils and a corresponding reduction in free centres like the Citizens' Advice bureaux that offer such a brilliant service to those who need financial advice, and Colin often needed help in this area.

Our holiday on Dartmoor in September 2017 was somewhat blighted by my opening some of Colin's letters for him just before we left. In the middle of the heap, but dated just a few days earlier, was a fine of £370 for nonpayment of TV licence, for non-attendance at a court hearing, and for not sending back the forms that had evidently been posted to him after he told the friendly man who knocked on his door one day that, yes he did have a 'telly'; and he had signed a form to say so as well. He said he never thought anything of it at the time! I wished he had told me.

Unfortunately, Denise had been ill and so the unopened post had accumulated, as Colin had deteriorating eyesight and couldn't read most of the letters without the help of a magnifying glass. He relied on Denise to sort them out for him as best she could. To be truthful as none of the letters ever contained good news, I'm pretty sure neither of them wanted to open the envelopes that piled up, making a useful mat for beer cans and coffee cups. I should have left the letter-opening till after the holiday! Once Colin realised who his inquisitive visitor had been and the trouble that was now ensuing, he sighed. 'It's all Fella's fault,' he remarked.

In a way it was. Delightful as Fella was, he did have one tendency that has also been remarked upon by my friend who later adopted him. Given the chance, he would run off and was not very inclined to return. Colin was walking him in a nearby copse of trees one evening in early summer 2017, when he tripped on a tree root and let go of the lead. Off Fella sped - transformed instantly from elderly limping terrier to streaking greyhound by the possibility of a few hours of freedom. Colin didn't have Fella's turn of speed, and the little dog was lost for two days. Luckily his name and address were on his collar, and he was picked up by the dog warden and returned. However, the dog rescue services had insisted on chipping him and also demanded what Colin called a 'ransom payment' for his return. The only place he could get the money from was the TV licence cash that was put away, as he paid it fortnightly. So, he handed it over.

This meant Colin was now £37 behind with his TV licence and struggling to make it up, so I offered to pay, but not directly to him, of course. After several days of searching, he found his licence number, and I went online and rang the TV licensing authority, only to find that this amount had been passed onto a debt collector and was no longer in their hands. £37 passed on to a debt collector! I rang the debt-collecting agency, and paid, using my debit card over the phone. I asked if that was the end of the matter, and was assured that it was, and that Colin didn't need to worry, and we could ignore any further letters about this.

I should have recorded that conversation. Because, far from being able to ignore any more letters, in September he received the already-mentioned letter from the court fining him £370 for this debt of £37 that had been paid several months earlier, and for not attending a court hearing, because he had as instructed been ignoring any more letters about the TV licence. It took many phone calls and emails for me to get anywhere near sorting this out.

Yet another letter was sent to him, and several months later Colin attended court and pleaded guilty to missing two licence payments and ignoring a court summons. Getting him to court involved booking a taxi and paying for it online and having a solicitor friend meet him at the court and support him throughout, making sure he didn't wander out for a drink or a smoke and not return.

He was fined £110 that he paid off over 20 weeks at £11 a fortnight. As he was reminded by the magistrate, not paying your TV licence is a criminal offence. It seemed to me that spending all this money taking someone to court for a £37 debt when it had already been paid was the crime. This caused many months of anxiety to my brother, for whom watching the television was fast becoming the only thing he was able to do. From then on I paid Colin's TV licence annually, as his birthday present.

If you have the means to pay this cost for your relative, it might be a good idea to do so, as any addict will put their own immediate needs before a TV licence payment. Though again, you may feel that you are treating them like a child or being over-controlling. This was a continual internal struggle for me: should I let Colin (who after all was an adult and only a few months younger than me) sink or swim, or should I be continually there with the life raft? Based on his huge recent loss of weight and learning from his eviction and homelessness during the years when I wasn't helping, I decided that I needed to try and keep him alive in the hope that one day he would be able to pull himself off the drugs. I could not bear it to be otherwise.

Bank accounts are another problematic area for those on benefits. For years benefits were paid into post office accounts, but as the number of post offices dwindled, getting there to collect them was becoming more difficult. The solution proposed by the government was to switch payment to bank accounts, and then the money could be drawn from any ATM. But these were also decreasing in number, a fact that wasn't mentioned.

Colin died last year as these measures were beginning to be introduced. The two post offices nearest him having closed down in the past few months, he was reliant on his increasingly unreliable dealer buddy to drive him four miles to the next one once a fortnight to collect his money. Of course, he charged a premium rate for petrol, and allowed Colin to buy him a few pints before they spent what remained of the money on whatever they could find in the drug line. Colin was not oblivious to the problems this created for him and would try and get two buses to collect his money but was often defeated by the half mile walk to the bus stop, especially in the cold weather.

He did have a bank account that he couldn't use. He was forced to open one when our uncle died and left him some money, which the solicitor would only pay by crossed cheque with his name on it into a personal bank account, much as Colin would have preferred the notes to have been counted out into his open hands! So, he opened an account with the Co-op bank in the nearest town. But this inheritance was spent super-quickly, and the account went into overdraft, and so was unusable for his benefits, which would have been swallowed up by the debt. He had regular letters from the bank that he added to his pile of unopened mail. There was no way he would be able to open another bank account or even use that one until the overdraft was cleared.

When I was in England I would drive Colin to the post office to get his money, and the only place we would go to spend any of it would be to the butcher to buy some liver and kidney and steak pies, which he loved. I also drove him to get his methadone (without of course requiring that he share it with me!) and I tried my best to get the doctor to pay a home visit and work out some way to relieve his breathing. In this last endeavour I was spectacularly unsuccessful. The doctor would not even make an appointment to call, as I describe later.

If Colin hadn't had his addictions, he would have had enough money to scrape by, though not enough to replace anything that broke, nor really enough to buy good warm clothes for the winter. But of course, alcohol and drugs cost money and were top of his concerns - way above food, rent or any other bills. So about 16 years ago I started buying Colin's groceries for him. I put in an online groceries order once a fortnight, mainly for the heavier items and also for emergency rations - tins of soup and stew and TV dinners that would keep him going if he couldn't get out. This was a difficult decision initially, as I didn't want Colin to become dependent on me for his day-to-day needs. However, feeding himself was way down on his list of priorities.

I have been criticized for this, even by his friend Denise, who was the first to shout her order for groceries down the phone and was equally happy to share Colin's food. People have told me that by providing his food I was leaving my brother with more spare money for drugs. True, but doing this meant that he always had enough to eat, didn't have to deal in order to afford drugs and was not getting his door or his face kicked in because of debts to dealers. On balance it seemed the best course, and I continued this right up to his death. It also decreased my worry. If Colin was too breathless to get out one day, at least he could open a tin of soup or have a cup of tea. And he didn't have to struggle home with heavy shopping bags.

Five years ago, when Colin inherited his small sum from our uncle, I was left substantially more money than this. This planted the seed of an idea in my head - rehab for Colin. Maybe I could persuade him to go to an alcohol and drug rehabilitation centre? I hesitated to even suggest it, but finally broached the subject when I next saw Colin. He wasn't angry or even particularly interested. He just looked at me hard, 'And who would be my friends then? What would I do with myself all day? Who would I hang out with?'

He had zoomed straight in on the heart of his problem: absolutely every one of Colin's friends had their own addiction to alcohol, and quite a few to heroin and cocaine as well. If he was to get clean, he would have to break his connections, and that was something he couldn't face.

Financial stress could also be generated by seemingly positive news. As I mentioned before, in June 2018 Colin began to live alone for the first time in many years. Initially all went well. The flat seemed ideal, and in some ways it was. It was freshly painted, light and airy. The outside door was secure, which meant there were no more 'friends' peering through the window, and popping in, to still be sleeping on the floor several days later because Colin hadn't had the heart to eject them. It was upstairs, with a lift, and the wind blew clear and clean across the tiny balcony that faced trees and overlooked well-tended gardens. The shower and toilet were adapted with all the handles that made life easier – and the 'red cord' that should never be pulled in error! He felt safer from dealers and unwanted guests. When he moved in, the flat contained a small Belling cooker, but no fridge or freezer and no other furniture. What little furniture Colin possessed stayed with Denise, so for the first few nights he ate back at his old home and slept in his new flat on a quilt on the floor, as he was scared of losing the place. 'If I don't take it, they'll give it to somebody else.'

Clothes were moved over in several shifts, by the trick of wearing them all one on top of the other and walking slowly between the two homes. My brother told me about it on the phone, 'Only time in my life I have ever looked fat!' We applied for an emergency loan from the local council to assist with buying furniture when he moved into his new place. A friend had given him an armchair and brought over the TV from his bedsit but he needed more to make this into a home. Again, I felt moved to help out, which was just as well, as there was never a reply to the emergency loan request. A charity also stepped in, and by August the flat had the bare (very bare) necessities. What happens to the person who doesn't have this support?

The second financial problem created a lot of anxiety for Colin. Three weeks after he moved in, he received letters demanding nearly £70 'owed rent'. He was in a panic, almost unable to breathe as he feared losing his new home. Luckily this was during one of my visits, and we set off to investigate, and organised an e-card to be used to pay the extra rent, and the appropriate reduction in council tax. It is not common knowledge that housing benefit does not necessarily cover the whole cost of sheltered housing, which tends to be more expensive than single rooms rented out by private landlords. Colin had a shortfall of over £23 a week to find for his rent, and about £16 extra a month for his council tax. He could manage the rent and I paid his council tax annually, but the worry it created stayed with him.

If you have a benefits-receiving relative or friend who is moving from one accommodation to another, they should let the housing benefits office know quickly, claim their council tax reduction and be sure to update their address for the TV licence. And if they don't know how to do any of this (and we didn't) go to the Citizen's Advice bureau or your local library and ask for help. There is a dreadful irony in that the government cuts that have hit benefits and made the system so complex have also reduced the funding for the services that help those struggling to stay afloat in the choppy waters!

Soon after Colin moved into his new flat I asked him if he was lonely. He replied that he liked his own company and there was nobody to boss him around.

'Except for you, of course,' he smiled.

CHAPTER SEVEN

DIGITAL BY DEFAULT

When the seemingly simple becomes impossibly complex

'Digital by default' is how the benefits system is described in the 2016 Ken Loach film 'I, Daniel Blake', which is about an unemployed man with health problems struggling to get the benefits to which he is entitled. The move to online sites when submitting claims and making appointments has been hugely problematic for those who are face-to-face by default. Colin was one of these. Everything he wanted to do required, in his view, that he visit an office and talk to somebody. But that is not how it works nowadays. Efforts to visit the housing office led us to a building that had been converted to 'housing officers only, no public' many years before. We were then directed to a branch office and found that we needed an appointment for several days ahead just to be able to talk to a housing officer. Nothing was easy.

I wonder how others manage in this digital age. It seemed to me my brother needed to move from face-to-face by default to at least telephone-and-pen by default. I bought him a mobile phone with large numbers and a clear display, which made things easier, but still wasn't enough to help him negotiate the many departments he needed to contact. The result was that benefits appointments were missed and payments delayed because of his inability to negotiate the system.

Moreover, government representatives wouldn't speak to me unless I was standing beside him and he gave verbal permission over the phone. As I only visited three or four times a year, this was unlikely to happen. Thus, the phone was no easier than being online, unless he could get to the fantastic Citizens' Advice bureau for help. Unfortunately, their part-time help desk was located in the library in the town centre, which was even further away than the post office and the bus stop or the nearest cashpoint. Nonetheless, when he could manage to visit there using his free bus pass and taking all the relevant forms and ID with him, they were always very helpful.

Sometimes Colin succeeded in getting a form sent to him. However, he often could not complete its many confusing pages. He would usually shove it in a drawer until I visited and we would fill it in together. Sometimes his requests got answered by mail, and sometimes they didn't. Phone calls would refer him to an online process for contacting the relevant authorities, and he would then give up.

The solution was for me to register Colin for an email address and also an online account with the council, so I could log in as him to keep an eye on things. I work online all day and every day, (digital by default!) and my brother was happy to share codes and passwords that he had been given, when he could find them. Just as I had previously searched online for several years to eventually find his sheltered accommodation, from 2018 I logged in weekly to check his rent had been paid and that there were no problems with his flat. I felt a little like a 'puppet master' behind the scenes. So much for not wanting to be controlling!

I was amused one day to come across an email from the local council housing department. The opening sentence warned that in future all correspondence from this department would be digital, through logging into your portal on their site, or by email. If you didn't want this to happen, you needed to reply to the email immediately, with your full name and address and tenancy agreement reference number, saying that you wished to still receive hard copies of letters through the post. Colin, so far as we were both aware, never received any intimation of this in a hard copy. I quickly answered that he wished to keep getting his housing correspondence through his letterbox, and this was agreed, in an email reply. But it is strange to email a person to ask them if they really need to receive hard copies of housing letters, as those who do are unlikely to see this e-correspondence!

Colin usually kept up with his rent and paid the excess over the post office counter every time he collected his benefit. If he lapsed, I would pay it online without telling him. By 2018 his thoughts were getting quite disorganised and this cognitive deterioration meant that he lost track pretty quickly, and so was not aware of his debts or of my help. Lapses in payments would usually coincide with illness and inability to go and claim his benefit. Colin owed just over £80 in back rent when he died, but by then I had been too concerned with his failing health to bother over anything else. But remember that, even if you are next-of-kin, you are not responsible for your relative's debts once they have passed away.

We once gave Denise and Colin an old but working laptop computer that would have connected to the internet, and on which they could have tried to develop some computer skills, but that too disappeared quite quickly from their little flat, with varying stories regarding what had happened to it: 'Pawned, lent to a friend, broke, around here somewhere.' I stopped asking.

But Colin didn't 'lose' everything I gave him. My first overseas job was in Thailand, and I brought him back an antique carved elephant puppet, which he succeeded in keeping safely for twenty-two years through all the house moves and pay-offs. I collected it from his flat when he had gone and took it back home with me.

I would have liked Colin to have been able to Skype me from the computer in the residents' lounge of his supported housing. He spoke about it several times, though it took me a while to understand what he meant when he said there was a 'spike' in the lounge that connected to the computer and we could telephone over it! However, every time I visited he said, 'Next time', suggesting he was too tired or distracted to give it a try.

I would ring him using my computer-to-phone Skype subscription, and this worked well, but of course it meant I couldn't see him. Colin didn't have a smart phone with screen, just a £10 Nokia from Tesco and the large-digit mobile phone with a stand that I had bought him, which he only used once or twice before it too disappeared. This meant I never saw him on-screen between visits and so every time I saw him in the flesh, his appearance was more and more of a shock.

I was continually worried about Colin's increasing inability to keep himself organised. He missed appointments, even the fortnightly one with the doctor at the Open Road organisation. This could be a disaster, as Colin needed to have a regular blood test there to prove he wasn't taking any other opiates before he could get his fortnightly script for methadone. I honestly don't know how he managed to 'pass' the blood test, but he always did.

I asked him what happened if he missed a blood test appointment. He replied that if worst came to worst he could always get hold of some methadone through friends. Evidently there is quite a black market in it! Now I understand why many addicts have to swallow it at the pharmacy in front of the staff, rather than being allowed to exit with a bottle. On reflection, Colin's life seemed incredibly complicated and demanding of someone in poor health.

CHAPTER EIGHT

STILL HOLDING MY BREATH

Just be there

Most of us only recognise a turning point in the life of someone we love after the turn has been taken. The fall and broken hip that signalled a downturn for our elderly uncle's health; the late onset diabetes that quickly resulted in amputations and illness for our mother and father; the surprise breast cancer that affected a younger friend so badly that she is still frightened even though she has been in remission for over three years. I recognised that my brother's turning point had come a few months after he moved to live by himself. It had become my practice to phone him before visiting, so he and Denise could tidy themselves and the little place where they lived.

However, a warning phone call made no difference very soon after he started living alone. He was slumped in front of the TV day and night and if Denise visited, she was shouted at if she so much as tried to wash a dish when the 'telly' was on, let alone vacuum the floor. It made me realise that perhaps she and Colin's previous girlfriend had done more cleaning than I gave them credit for. The guilt would well up in me as my feet stuck to the small spot of carpet that wasn't covered in junk, and I often decided to refuse a coffee when the flat was like this, as I didn't fancy needing the loo. I would have loved to help Colin have a good clear out, even though he had only been in his new flat a few months. He habitually collected other people's junk and throwaways as well as his own, and every surface was covered in dust, beer cans, ashtrays and his knick-knacks that 'might be worth something one day.'

But several things eventually stopped me from offering to clear up: firstly, it would take away from precious time we could have spent chatting. With his COPD, Colin would have needed to leave the flat due to the dust and dirt that would be kicked up, and secondly, it was his home, and drawing attention to the state it was in felt as if I was insulting him. I would take bags of rubbish downstairs to the communal bins as I left. I offered to hire a small van and do a few trips to the dump but the response was always, 'Oh, it's not so bad really.'

Another reason that I didn't intrude was that I was afraid what I would find. This made me feel ashamed, but it was a fact. I had been clearing up one day during his first few weeks in the flat and when I still felt hopeful that he would make it on his own. I opened the kitchen drawer in which he kept his housing letters and various bills, to check if there was anything that needed paying.

'Oh,' I thought as I spied some tinfoil lying in the top of the drawer. 'He's changed his kitchen around. This has his cooking stuff in it now.'

But then I saw the official envelopes lying underneath, pushed the tinfoil aside, and pulled them out. I realised that the square of tinfoil had been hiding beneath it a burnt-looking plastic tube belonging to a biro, a couple of battered spoons and a lighter - crack cocaine gear. I closed the drawer, and felt my legs shake. I went through the letters and bills and never mentioned this to Colin, but from then on decided to ask him to get any letters out before I came.

The fact that Colin didn't feel up to much washing of the flat or himself signalled something about his health, his breathing, his energy levels and his mental state. Unable to even get to the bus stop except on a very good day, he was really trapped now. So my visits increasingly revolved around chasing up what he was due moneywise, and having conversations about our childhood, his current friends, the daily doings of others in his little block of flats and general chit-chat. As Colin became more ill and immobile, his previous friends dropped away quickly and he was often not visited for days on end. However, Denise was loyal and stayed with him in the flat once he became more incapacitated, looking after him to the best of her ability, which varied from day to day, as she had her own addiction problems.

If and when he sat and thought about our afternoons together, I wanted him to remember the love and friendship, not feel embarrassed about the dirt, or sad because I had judged him. The time for that had long passed. The turning point had come. No holiday with us was possible after 2017, though we still got out for brief car rides whenever he was able.

Soon after the realisation hit me that Colin had really reached the point of no return and was going downhill fast, I snapped him smiling outside his new place, in August 2018. This, apart from a private photo I took in hospital which is just for me, is the last photo of Colin that exists. It is in stark contrast with the photos taken in Dartmoor and Devon just eleven months earlier. He had come a long way in a year, and none of it in the right direction.

August 2018

My sixty-fifth birthday came around in September 2019, and I invited my brother to lunch at a pub restaurant just outside Colchester, with Uwe, my sons and their families and a few friends. I knew he wouldn't come, because eating in front of others was impossible - he had to mash and liquidise everything by then, as swallowing was becoming increasingly difficult. But to receive the invitation as a family member meant a lot and he knew he would have been welcome. Instead, Uwe and I took him a few days later to the small seaside town where we grew up, for a swift drink looking out over the sea. I was shocked by how much weight he had lost, even in the month since I last saw him and begged him to go to the doctor's. But the fear of being admitted to hospital and not having access to his beer and drugs prevented him from doing that.

In late October I came over to see Colin again and the minute I saw him I wanted to ring an ambulance. Wheezing in the chair, he was blue and breathless, but he was refusing Denise's entreaties to go to hospital. I joined the campaign of persuasion, but to no avail. Colin became very agitated and swore he would refuse to get in the ambulance even if we did ring the emergency services. I called round again the next day, only to find a distraught Denise alone in the flat. Of course, it was benefit day. My brother's dealer friend had turned up uninvited, helped him get dressed and driven him to get his money. Denise was crying, but his friend's and his need for whatever they could both buy was greater than his pain. I left, feeling furious and frustrated.

Two days later, I drove Colin to the pharmacy to get his methadone, before heading out for the airport for my return trip home. I had time to talk to him alone about his terrible health, and finally, my brother agreed to let me ring the doctor and ask him to visit the next morning. The new receptionist didn't know Colin, and was helpful, insisting the doctor would call round straight after morning surgery. I breathed a sigh of releief.

He didn't come. Instead, Colin got a phone call early the next day saying the doctor would not attend him at home, as he continually failed to keep surgery and hospital appointments. If he couldn't get himself to the surgery and sit in the waiting room for several hours or be organised enough to make an appointment and be well enough to catch the bus there, then there was no way he would get to see a doctor. He couldn't do any of this, and so my attempt to get him some care came to nothing.

According to Denise, Colin protested strongly over the phone, but to no avail. I was incensed, but by then he was confirmed in his opinion that the medical profession just didn't care. Addicts are often treated like this, but it compounds their mistrust, and who can blame them? A few days earlier I had asked Denise privately to ring 999 for an ambulance if Colin ever became unconscious. She looked doubtful but agreed. After my return to Portugal I started ringing Colin every day, persisting until either Denise or he answered the phone. Some days he sounded better than others and I began to believe that maybe we had some time left together.

But in mid-November the inevitable happened: Colin became dehydrated and confused and on point of collapse. Denise had panicked and phoned his key worker at the STaRS alcohol and drug support service. They called Colin's GP practice and insisted on a visit. A more sympathetic doctor had attended and had rung an ambulance the moment she took a look at my brother and Colin was rushed to hospital. This was a Friday evening, and I happened to ring his phone, which he had left behind, just after the ambulance took him away. Denise was sobbing and quite incoherent. For some reason she had not gone with him, so knew no more than me.

My youngest son, who lives fairly near the hospital, drove there to find out what was happening. Meanwhile I telephoned, to be told they had no record of his admission. The kind receptionist investigated further and found he was still in the ambulance as they were trying to resuscitate him. By the time my son arrived, his Uncle Colin had been admitted to the emergency resuscitation area, where he drifted into consciousness long enough to give a thumbs up to his anxious nephew.

The admitting doctor had questions: 'Is Colin an alcoholic?'

'Yes.'

'A drug user?'

'Yes.'

'Diabetic?'

Quick phone call to me. 'Not as far as we know.'

'Is anyone coming - partner or other relative?'

'Yes, my Mum's his sister, and she'll come.'

'Tell her to get here quickly. We'll do our best, but your uncle's very ill.'

I don't know why Denise didn't go to the hospital with Colin on that Friday night. Naturally it all happened at speed, and of course she wouldn't have been completely sober by that time in the evening, so maybe it was just as well. I told her I would come straight away, but it might be late the next afternoon before I arrived. Not for the first time, I wished I lived much nearer to my brother.

I dashed to the airport on that Saturday in November to catch the early morning Heathrow flight via Lisbon. Throughout my journey, Denise rang continually to ask when I was arriving. She had visited Colin in the hospital and was still there but kept telling me she was 'in pieces' and 'needed a break.' She was popping outside for a smoke and swig from the bottle of cider that was a permanent fixture in her inside jacket pocket, and that's when she was calling me. Once she left the phone on accidentally and I could hear her mumbling to herself as she became more and more distressed. I pressed the button to cut her off. Colin I could deal with, but a drunk Denise was another matter.

My two sons had been in to visit during the morning, and I got more sense out of them. Colin was on a ward and conscious, but still in grave danger from complications of pneumonia and with severe liver damage. He was on oxygen, had extremely low blood pressure and couldn't really speak. It was after 7 pm by the time I arrived, straight from the train station with my youngest son. Denise was sitting outside the hospital on a bench looking upset and exhausted and definitely the worse for alcohol. She rejected my son's offer of a lift home after he had visited, saying she had booked a taxi, but couldn't bear to go back into the ward, and needed a day off. We went in.

I decided to stay with Colin as long as I could. Visiting hours were waived and we kept each other company throughout the Saturday night. My first job was to sniff at the two bottles of Lucozade in prime position on his tray table. One was the real sugary stuff but the other was flat beer, which had been half drained. Evidently Denise had thought she was being kind again, but the staff had already told me they were giving him medication to ease the alcohol withdrawal so drinking much of this would make him sick. Followed by Colin's eyes, I took it away and gave it to the ward sister, with a request that they keep their eyes open for more arriving via visitors. I needn't have worried. It was forty-eight hours before I saw Denise again, and no other friends visited at all. This gave us another problem: it was the weekend, and Colin needed his methadone, which had been left behind in the flat. Denise sent a photo of the bottle for the ward sister, with the dosage on it, but the prescribing doctor needed to see the real thing before he was willing to give any to Colin. Denise wasn't coming in to visit for a day, so I arranged for my son to step into the breach again and collect the methadone from Colin's flat early the next morning.

In the dark ward, I rubbed cream gently into the split and itchy skin on Colin's back. His bony shoulder blades and heaving ribs reminded me of the baby birds we used to find fallen from the nest when we were children.

We would run home with them and put each carefully in a shoe box and try and feed it with milk and chopped-up worms. Then we would bury it a day or two later in its cardboard coffin, as they always died. The similarity was painful.

It was hard to know where to touch Colin without hurting him. I turned him carefully and helped him drink water throughout the long dark hours. The armchair was uncomfortable, and there were no spare pillows to be found anywhere. I could hardly borrow one of the four that were propping up Colin! Neither of us slept much, but he was very thirsty, and drank the whole contents of the water jug a tiny glass at a time. He couldn't talk a lot, because of his shortness of breath. But most of his attention was focused on his desperate needs. At about midnight I rang the bell and was able to find a nurse who gained the authority to give Colin something more to take the edge off his craving for alcohol, but she could do nothing about his rising demands for methadone. I promised it would be with him in the morning.

In the early hours he lapsed into a restless sleep, waking with a jerk at about 6 am. 'I need my methadone,' he told me angrily. 'It's coming soon,' I tried to reassure him. He sighed, drank water, and settled back on the pillows. That was the last conversation I had with my brother. When the breakfast trolley came around an hour later there was no rousing him. He was now unconscious, and I hadn't even noticed. I had thought he was getting the sleep he needed at last!

Unlike Colin's regular GP, the hospital doctors and nurses were sympathetic and kind, but there was no returning from this. He was sixty-three years old and ravaged by his addictions and illness that had reduced him to a skeleton in a parchment skin. Twice I overheard a meals assistant ask, 'What about the old man in the side ward - Colin?' The words jolted me, though they were true. My leather-jacketed, denim-jeaned younger brother was a dying old man.

Denise returned to the hospital on Monday afternoon, and we kept an uneasy joint vigil by his bedside. She became more drunk and increasingly loud and belligerent, somehow blaming and resenting me in equal measures, and then apologizing profusely, before starting to mutter angrily again. Luckily she would often wander off around the hospital on one or other mission - to get a phone card, find a cup of coffee, or go outside for a cigarette. It was a relief to me when she took a half hour break to go to the nearby shop for more cider. She also didn't stay at night, and wouldn't reappear until late afternoon the next day, so I was there peacefully with my brother for the quiet hours. I moistened his mouth with sponges on sticks, played the radio to him and me, and realised that there really was little more to be done for him. I was alone with Colin when he died early in the morning two days later and it was peaceful, at least looking in from the outside, for what do we really know?

How do family members deal with the guilt when their relative finally dies, far too young? We all feel we could have done more when someone we love has gone.

But the pull was much too strong for me to stop it. Being there as your relative lives and as they die and loving them unconditionally is hard to do but seems the only road possible.

Although Colin died a year ago now, I am still holding my breath. He is still with me. My dreams are of me as a child chasing through the woods, looking for Colin, only to find him as an adult slumped and drugged, lying against a tree. I am aware of the symbolism of this, and try and extend it when awake, picturing myself sitting there beside him, talking to him and kissing him, as indeed I was when the end came.

I have a few photographs and some memories of happier times. They are worth a lot, considering how painful his last few weeks were. But I still feel guilty. I could not protect my 'little brother' from himself, or the dealers and pseudo-friends who would help him to collect his benefits and his methadone but wouldn't take him to his necessary hospital appointments.

The last gift I gave Colin was his funeral. Though of course a funeral is really for yourself and those who remember the person who has gone. While preparing this, I was thinking about his life 'on the edge' and wrote a poem for the service. Maybe it will help those family members going through the same as me to feel a little better. There are many of us.

THE LAST STEP

I always lived on, looked over, hovered too near the edge.
Friends would pull me back, or occasionally urge me on.
Sometimes my vision blurred, and the edge called me.

I promised 'Never again' and turned away from the edge.
But when I looked round it changed shape and beckoned me
Into warm waters, a soft caressing sea.

In my daydreams and night terrors I roamed the edge Until
my feet began to slip and I couldn't get away.
I listened to the call and stepped off the edge.

EPILOGUE

Know your limits

Reading back through this book I realise that it could just as easily read as 'How not to do it.' I thought to go back and change some sentences. But you can't change what happened, and my learning from reflection is too late for Colin. But I hope others may look to it for possible insight into a difficult journey and ideas of what to do, or what not to do.

Finally, while sitting with Denise by Colin's deathbed and dealing with her moods and outbursts, I also learnt my limits. I resolved to pay for the funeral. I suggested that Denise chose three songs for the crematorium service. I introduced her, and the few of Colin's friends who turned up for the service, to his son Steven and Steven's wife Karen and to our elderly cousins.

I shared Colin's ashes with her. Then I went back to Portugal and deleted her phone number.

I also deleted the number of Colin's friend who took him to collect his money and his methadone and shared in both. I deleted the number of his previous landlord who lent him cash, turned a blind eye to his meter-fiddling and came to his funeral. The only connection I kept was with Steven and Karen and their three little boys whom I contact regularly. Something good had to come from all of this.

Colin was my brother and I loved him. But I could not take on his addict friends and their needs. I could not even keep contact with Denise who had tried in her own way to help. They have their own relatives, and maybe one of them one day will read this book and recognize the role they could fulfill in supporting their loved one.

Colin 2013

Walking along a city street in the south-west of England at Christmas 2019, a few weeks after Colin's death, I waited to cross at the lights. There in front of me was Colin - gasping and bent in a scuffed and frayed leather jacket with a cigarette butt in his mouth. The man turned slightly and, of course it wasn't Colin, and nor was the one sitting in a sleeping bag on the other side of the road, or that one on the bench with his beer.

So many 'not Colins'. He is gone and yet he is everywhere, and this was when I realised that I had to write our story.

UK ORGANISATIONS FOR RELATIVES AND FRIENDS OF ADDICTS

Addictions UK
5a Station Terrace
East Boldon
Tyne and Wear NE36 0LJ
Tel: 0800 1404044
Website: www.addictionsuk.com
Services for those addicted as well as family and friends affected. Not just for drug/alcohol addiction.

Adfam
Tel: 0203 817 9410
Website: www.adfam.org.uk
Provides local family support services.

Al-Anon Family Groups UK & Eire
57B Great Suffolk Street
London SE1 0BB
Tel (Helpline): 0800 0086 811
Website: www.al-anonuk.org.uk/
Confidential support and mentoring for families and also for friends.

Drugfam
Tel (Helpline): 0300 888 3853
Website: www.drugfam.co.uk
Provide support for family, partners and friends affected by someone's drug and/or alcohol use, including those who have been bereaved.

Mind
15-19 Broadway
Stratford E15 4BQ
Tel (SANEline): 0300 304 7000
Website: www.mind.org.uk/
For those experiencing problems or those supporting others with mental health problems.

Open Road
12 North Hill
Colchester CO1 1DZ
Tel: 01206 766096
Website: www.openroad.org.uk
Drug and alcohol support services.

STaRS Colchester (Open Road)
5A Queen Street
Colchester CO1 2PG
Tel: 01206 710757
Both Open Road and the affiliated STaRS deal mainly with addicts but are also a great support to relatives and friends.

The Forward Trust
Edinburgh House
170 Kennington Lane
London SE11 5DP
Tel: 0203 981 5525
Website: www.forwardtrust.org.uk/
Community drug and alcohol services for addicts and their families.